# TODAY
# HAMLET

Natalie Shapero

**Out-Spoken Press**
London

Published by Out-Spoken Press,
PO Box 78744
London, N11 9FG

A CIP record for this title is available from the British Library.

First edition published 2023
ISBN: 978-1-7392652-6-7

Typeset in Adobe Caslon
Design by Patricia Ferguson
Printed and bound by Print Resources

Out-Spoken Press is supported using public funding by the National
Lottery through Arts Council England.

Supported using public funding by
ARTS COUNCIL
ENGLAND

*'César Vallejo has died.'*

— César Vallejo (trans. Rebecca Seiferle)

*for the Californians*

# Contents

# Red Item

I don't smoke. I know it's dangerous, I say now
of the sun instead, but I shun the advice to avoid it.
I just have to have it right on me. I feel bad

for the people in the movie where the ovular vessels
from outer space cause a shadow
over all of Los Angeles. It's not the sun

we need less of. It's the moon. Less of its blankness.
Less of its compliance. Its wholesomeness.
Its spotless beam. Like a work shirt. I feel bad

for the laundromat in the movie where one red item
is washed with a load of lights. It's bad
to have that in you. The moment when everything's ruined.

## First of January

Faces change. Wavelengths fade. Staying in
is the new going out and dying
is the new staying in. Don't waste your time
drinking water: those wells
just laze around all day getting wished on
by the sinister; then every night,
they're granting, granting, granting.
Let's remove to the desert. Let's
get into acting. Let's get
really natural. Let's get dead. Yeah Happy
New Year. Don't let it go to your head.

# A Little Late for That

It is a plain fact of insomnia that anyone
who endures it for sufficient duration will never truly experience
the phenomenon of night. When asked how long

I have worked at my job, I truthfully answer ONE DAY.
One enormous day. I do not sleep
                                because when you come back
from the dead, I don't want to miss it. And, if we're
being honest, I would also prefer not to miss it

when I come back from the dead. Yeah I assume we can all agree
I must have died at some prior point, seeing as this world
is Hell. It's Hell, and I wander it
                                as though in someone else's
dream. They keep insisting they see me. I don't agree.

# This Poem is Called a Little Late for That

As I've said, I'm convinced that this world
is Hell, and the conviction makes me desperate

to somehow reconstruct the prior place
from which we were dispatched. I don't have memories

of it, but I can sense its heft, and sometimes
I get cold and I swear
I've stumbled into the shadow of its obverse side.
It has a presence,

the way Mark Rothko argued a painting
ought to have a presence, so that when you turn your back

to the canvas, you continue to feel it,
feel it like your skin can feel the sun. It has a presence,

the way the ill man waking
in the night could feel his long-dead father, and he readied
himself to be led right out of his body
and into the world that's next, but instead

he got two ghost hands pressing his chest
down into the bed and toward the dirty earth: NOT YET.

# First of August

I wouldn't say I had no childhood.

I wouldn't say, for example, that I've experienced anything as extreme
as the scene in Mary Shelley's FRANKENSTEIN
where the creature, eavesdropping on a tutoring session
concerning human development, finds he can retrieve no memory
of ever being small, amplifying his crisis of identity. What am I.

What I would say is that it was detected

in me at a very young age that I was destined to be a ghost.
Apparently you can just tell. Some people are merely
passing through. Some people are hardly here. I read about

the pathbreaking teacher of acting who, when asked
why he never greeted students while sidling by them in the hall, said
WHAT IS THERE TO SAY HELLO ABOUT?

Washing my hands in a public bathroom, I see other people seeing me

as I look at myself in the mirror, and I feel them
scorning my gaze. WHAT DOES SHE HAVE TO LOOK
IN THE MIRROR ABOUT?

## Lithol Red

Truly, it is not good to be an actor. It is better
to be a painter, to be something
with the potential to have one's work degraded by the sun.
To really fear it. I practice at home
with fruit. I set them on the sill for weeks
and observe them turning sallow. Worst is the tomato.
I see myself in its red. It demands
its own kind of knife. It's so prissy. Just for once get cut,
why don't you, with what cuts everyone else—

## It's Done

I have killed exactly one man. I have birthed exactly
one baby. I birthed the baby to replace the man I killed, make
whole the halting world. In the halting world, I have made
myself at home. A lot of heating up soup and knotting

the strands of little string bags. Repeating conventional wisdom
regarding the speed with which a new car loses
value once it's driven off the lot. Watching films in which a hit man

telephones a financier and simply says IT'S DONE. This happens
over and over. Okay, okay, you got me. I birthed
a baby, but I never killed a man. I can't even change

a tyre. Did you really think I could take him? YOU SHOULD SEE,
I said, THE OTHER GUY, but that's more
of an expression. Seeing as no one
saw him. Seeing as no one saw him ever again.

# Sell-Off

haven't you noticed you aren't the president I sometimes
and fully unfairly feel like saying when people in personal capacities
opine on incoming horrors my THOUGHTS GO OUT
TO THE FAMILIES AND ALL IMPACTED haven't you noticed
that no one expects you to soothe and condemn that no one
is watching the clock asking when will you step up though also
who really am I to opine on who is and who isn't
the president when I myself after being near-murdered made
near-constant jokes like some president steadying wall street asserting
his pluck and heartiness and so forestalling a sell-off who am I
kidding if I were to never recover the market
would hold horribly firm they could wheatpaste
every phone pole in this city with my photo
and in large print NATALIE BOBBIE SHAPERO WILL NEVER
RECOVER and no one would lose let me tell you even a dime

## We Don't Want Any

Sometimes when I answer the door to a knocking
friend, I like to pretend
I assume it's a stranger come to make a sale. WE DON'T WANT ANY.
It's so tired but I keep
it up. Commitment is a virtue. Also I basically
mean it. Don't console me with the latest. Don't
ply me with novelty. BECAUSE OF MY HISTORY, I say to my lover,
then feel displeased by the blank embrace
of proprietary phrasing. BECAUSE OF MY HISTORY. Why would I
frame it, when I hate it, as something I own? It surprises me
any time I hear someone say the words MY RAPIST.
The sheer incorporation. TAKE MY RAPIST, PLEASE. You have to
commit to the bit. To my lover, I say BECAUSE OF HISTORY—

# Suddenly

the cause they never
volunteered and we never asked and everyone
knew what that meant

what they said was SUDDENLY

making his end sound epiphanic, the apple
beaning Isaac Newton or keen Scheherazade attuning

to the stupefying force of narrative, THE ONLY
WEAPON WE HAVE

I've read those stories
tyrants in vindictive fervour, taking it out
on dogs and servants

the accrual of despair in the world of whim
less sudden it couldn't have been

# Here and Only Here

You know what they say: TODAY HAMLET,
TOMORROW A SUPERNUMERARY. You know
what they say: today planet Earth, tomorrow
consignment to Hell. I've had enough

with these people who feel so superior
to the dead all the time. Who flaunt their beats
and pulses. Who ostentatiously obsess
over things only living people know of,

the origin of the word ENDEMIC
or the overrepresentation, in movies and TV,
of one red item going through
the wash with a load of lights. Although, trust me,

it does happen. It happens more than you think.
Weddings, blessings, laboratories.
Fencing, tennis, hotel kitchens.
Painters on their scaffold towers. Pink.

## Laundry Day

Seeing my neighbour in the zip-up bearing
the name of her employer even
on her day off IT'D BETTER BE
LAUNDRY DAY I'm thinking with the cadence

like when B died and L in the kitchen
after the service said THERE'D
BETTER BE A HEAVEN as though lodging
a threat against God I do believe

there's a Heaven but come on like everything else
they're offering surely it's only temporary
surely our dead will soon be struck
from the afterlife and then we will have

a new grief beyond any former grief
with the dead having been made dead in a way
never known before no mumbling
to them in the gorges no sensing their presence

beside the sequoias not even in dreams
will we find them you think you've known death
but you haven't time's ticking what little you have
to convey to your dead do it now

## Who Died and Made You

king I'm pretty
sure he was about to say or possibly
president but some coughing
hit him before he could finish and he ducked
away for water and we were left with WHO DIED

AND MADE YOU as though we are creating
one another when we die and I guess I'm sorry

to or about the person who didn't get to get made
that time when it seemed I was headed for an ending but—
suprise!—I pulled through

I imagine that person in that instant unforming
and who was she or who would
she have become

maybe she would have been better for the planet
maybe she would have been the type to isolate
the gene that would otherwise end you
in which case may I offer you
an apology for my continued existence it's weird

it's like I can see her

raising her chemical-resistant
goggles and squinting straight down at the burner
adjusting her unblemished coat and keying
in progress and saving
your sorry life

## Nightmare Is Putting It Mildly

I shouldn't become an actor. I should
become a painting. I want to be able to argue for myself
to be put in dark storage, make my point by blanching
in sunlight. I embrace the field of art history,
though I struggle with the overrepresentation,
in scholarly articles, of one red Rothko
getting put through the wash with a load of lights.
My least favorite term of endearment
is STRANGER, used to demonstrate
affection and at the same time rebuke
the beloved for their remove. It's only appropriate
to use when addressing celestial bodies. The Earth
as seen from space. The moon. The moon.

## Rock Creek Park

I know too much about too much. I don't
want to. I don't want to know about Hartford
being the insurance capital
of North America. Same goes for the official dish
of Louisville, the Hot Brown.
I don't want to know about anyone
being surreptitiously buried
in Rock Creek Park. I would rather
not have the information
that, in Southern California, you
GO TO THE SEASONS, meaning that the heat
and the blooms and the snow can all exist
simultaneously; at one elevation,
it's winter, at another it's summer and another
it's spring and you feel
which one you need and then you go.
So where, I said to Roxi,
is it always fall? She said that would be
difficult, for a place to remain in continuous fall,
and of course she was correct.
Nothing can stay suspended in decline
for so long without going fully
gone. I don't want to know. But don't I know.

# Acknowledgements

Thank you to tremendous Californians Becky Alexander, Roxi Carter, Sarah Gilbert, Lindsay Gilmour, Rebecca Morgan Frank (honorary), Kristy Hanselman, Paul Hanselman, Kerry Howley, Jess Lacher, Michelle Latiolais, Ted Martin, Jake Marmer, Annie McClanahan, Anahid Nersessian, Shoshana Olidort, Zoë Reyes, Chris Seeds, Meg Shevenock, Braxton Sonderman, Claire Vaye Watkins, Monica Youn, Pony Sweat Aerobics, Pioneertown, all my students, and the children of the aforementioned adults. And R. And F. And Martha.

Thank you to the University of California, Irvine. Thank you to Anthony Anaxagorou, Wayne Holloway-Smith, Patricia Ferguson, and all at Out-Spoken Press. Thank you to Michael Wiegers and Copper Canyon Press.

# Selected other titles by Out-Spoken Press

Email: press@outspokenldn.com